Booked

The digital marketing and socialmedia
appointment setting system for anyone
looking for a steady stream of leads,
appointments, and new clients.

Dedications are usually reserved for people that have influenced the author over the years. This time, I'd like to dedicate this book to only one person.

You.

I dedicate this book to you. Your commitment to growing your business is what makes this book possible. We may not yet know each other, or maybe we do. Either way, it is you who this book is for.

Thank you!

Want a **FREE VIDEO TRAINING** of the Booked System?

By purchasing this book, you're entitled to a companion video series by Josh Turner, at no extra charge. In these videos, you'll get an in-depth breakdown of the 5 pillars of the Booked system.

Get your videos at:

TheBookedBook.com/Videos

TABLE OF CONTENTS

INTRODUCTION

You're reading this book. So that means a couple things.

For starters, you're a human. Me too! Welcome to the club!

I bet you're also a human with a business, a business you'd like to grow. That makes two of us. It's great to have you in that club too.

Maybe you're just starting your business. Maybe you started your business years ago.

You might have a modest amount of income coming in. You might have no income quite yet. Or you might be a bit more established, with multiple six, seven, or eight figures of revenue.

Wherever you fall on that spectrum, we all have one thing in common. In order to get your next client, you must first get your next lead. There's no other way around it. Without a "lead", it is almost impossible to sign a paying client. And the only way to land your next client (and the next one, and the next one...) is to position yourself in front of your prospects, convert a percentage of them into leads, schedule appointments, and turn at least one of them into a client.

It really is that simple. But if you're paying too much attention to all the gurus, maybe you're feeling a bit like I was when I first started my business. Overwhelmed and uncertain about which strategies and tactics will work for you.

What I want you to do right now is get rid of all that noise. Set it all aside. Let's focus on the simple truth about what it takes to grow your business. Here's the framework one more time:

A. Position yourself in front of your prospects.

B. Convert a percentage of these prospects into leads and appointments.

C. Turn at least one of them into a client.

You're likely thinking to yourself at this very moment, "Yeah Josh, that's not rocket science. Tell me something I don't already know." And you're absolutely right! However, chances are you're not currently doing a good enough job on A and B to get enough C.

But that's ok, and seriously…you shouldn't blame yourself. I've seen it time and time again.

You have an amazing business, you do awesome work, and your clients love you. When you get a prospect on the phone, or you sit down face-to-face, there's a good chance they're going to do business with you. But you simply are not getting enough opportunities.

What good is the best home run hitter, if he never

gets an at-bat? You can't hit the ball, if you don't have enough at-bats. You're a home run hitter. If you weren't, you wouldn't be reading this book. You just need more at-bats.

Like I said, I've seen it time and time again.

The first time I saw it, I was 22.

ONE

FISHING, DRYWALL, AND FAILURE

I was fortunate to grow up in a loving and supportive family. My Dad was a typical American father figure. Tough but loving. Most importantly, he taught me to fish from a very young age.

That's me in the diapers, my Dad in the hat. It doesn't get better than this.

When I was just a few years old, I remember Dad remodeling our basement. He had learned on his own how to build stuff. And was very good at it. At the time, he was working for a big insurance company. Less than 10 years later, in a story that is all too familiar to most of us, he was downsized. And the prospect of getting another "job" was not only daunting, it was unattractive.

After a long and successful career working for other people, and being unceremoniously kicked to the curb, Dad was itching to chart his own path. To dive into the dream, and start his own business.

When I was about 13, he took his self-taught knowledge of remodeling basements and set out on his own. Before long, his newly founded business would provide me with an opportunity that would change my life.

Within a couple years, Dad started getting me involved in the business. I'd meet him after school sometimes to help out with a job. He started teaching me some of the basics. He showed me how to hang doors and install baseboard, and sometimes I'd be "lucky" enough to carry drywall up and down flights of stairs. Grueling, but not as grueling as holding a piece of drywall up while it's being screwed to a ceiling.

In 1999 I headed off to college at University of Missouri, and would work for him during the summer when I came home. My responsibilities increased, and by the time I was 22 I wasn't just a trim carpenter. I was helping estimate jobs, coordinating schedules with subcontractors, managing projects, communicating with clients, helping out with marketing and sales, and basically whatever he needed help with. Dad's business had grown to the point where he had several jobs going at any given time. And one year he even reached the $1 million revenue mark.

He had boats, nice cars, went on nice vacations. He worked when he wanted to and seemingly had all the freedom in the world. One of my favorite perks, he had season tickets to the St. Louis Blues. From my viewpoint, he had it all.

We had talked about me working for him full-time once I got done with school. My mind was made up. That's what I planned on doing. Working with my Dad and helping him grow the family business.

Then one day in 2002, he asked me to come into his office and told me that he had no choice but to shut down the business. Things had turned south. Work opportunities had dried up. The projects he had on the books were all wrapped up. There was no more money coming in. And because the preceding few months had become increasingly slow, the payables had started to mount. As the business lost money, the debt mounted. And the hole was too big to dig out of. Unable to pay the bills, he had no choice but to shut the doors.

It was a jolt to my system. I expected this was my future. Now it was gone.

For Dad, it became one of the most difficult times of his life. The business he built was gone, and he was forced to consider going back to working for somebody else. It had a huge financial toll of course, but the emotional toll of failing was even greater.

How could this have been avoided? It's possible that cutting costs and spending less could have kept the business more profitable in the years leading up to it. But the deficit was too great and it would have only delayed the inevitable.

The only thing that could have prevented Dad's business from going under? More opportunities, leads and clients. You can't grow by cutting costs. The only way to grow, or to remain stable, is to generate a consistent flow of leads.

As I said in the previous chapter, it's simple. The only way to get more clients is to get in front of more prospects. To schedule more appointments, consultations, strategy sessions, sales calls…whatever you want to call it. More appointments, more sales. If you want more business, your calendar needs to start filling up. Soon enough, when a prospect asks if you can talk tomorrow…you'll have to tell them you're booked. When your calendar fills up with appointments, you can start to pick and choose who you work with, raise your prices, make more money, and succeed in the game of business.

Dad didn't have the marketing systems in place to guarantee enough appointments. While times were good, he did well. But when things slowed down, without this system his business went under.

Fortunately, Dad rebounded a few years later to start another business and continues to run that business. He's now nearing retirement and is looking forward to a few more years of hard work, and booking a lot of appointments on his calendar.

TWO

TRAGEDY AWAITS

After my Plan A failed, I landed a new job at Boa Construction in January 2004.

Boa was a company doing about $5 mm in revenue, with two divisions. One was Boa Construction, a custom homebuilder and remodeling firm. The other side of the company was Architectural Millwork of St. Louis, a cabinet and millwork manufacturer.

I was in charge of the finance department and did a lot of other stuff there.

In just a few short years, we went from $5 million to over $23 million in annual revenue!

From the outside, it looked like a very successful business. But on the inside, we were living paycheck to paycheck.

When times were good, we had a lot of work. But in 2008 when things got more competitive in the market, our sales team couldn't find any new business. We ran out of work. And one day, we realized we couldn't afford to keep the lights on any more.

And that was it. In 2009, the company was forced to shut its doors. This was the second time in 10 years that I had been a part of a company that failed, because we weren't able to generate enough new business.

It was one of the lowest moments of my life. I felt like a total failure, and the business I was so proud to have been a part of...it was simply gone.

I was like so many other people...cast aside by the corporate world, and out on my own. Sure, I could've looked for another JOB, but I was tired of working for other people.

Not only that, but I had learned an important lesson for the second time.

The most important thing for any business is marketing and sales.

Without enough leads, your business is in jeopardy. It's imperative that you build a system to generate a consistent flow of opportunities in good times and in bad.

With that in mind, I resolved to setting out on my own.

THREE

SLEEPLESS NIGHTS

I started my business in early 2010. At the time, I was a 29 year old, unemployed, finance guy. And I didn't have a great image of myself. After all, I had just played a big part in the failure of a $23 million company. Who was I to run a business?

Countless entrepreneurs have shared with me that they felt much the same way when they first got started. Like a fraud. But we all have something else in common too. We push through that fear, because we know that working for somebody else just isn't in the cards anymore.

So that's exactly what I did. With my finance background and a LinkedIn rolodex of about 500 contacts, I decided to call myself an "outsourced CFO." I created a terrible looking website and had some business cards made at Kinko's. They were terrible too. But I was in the game.

I was fortunate to land my first client within a couple weeks. It was a real stroke of luck for me, but the company that hired me felt the same way. I dove in and delivered great value for them.

But with only 1 client, the feelings of being a fraud were growing. When you only have one client, you feel like you barely even have a real business. Yet you have no other choice but to parade around town acting like you have a real business. I mean, if you tell people about your fears, most of them will be completely turned off, right? Better to act strong and confident so they can have the same confidence in you.

That's how we all act when first starting out. But, unless you're a narcissist, it creates a tremendous amount of tension inside of you. You feel like a bit of a fraud. You feel less than "good enough" because you see other people with big successful businesses, and you know that yours is nothing close to theirs. You want your peers to respect you. You want your friends to respect you. You want your family to respect you. But deep down, you're afraid that you're failing on all counts.

This story runs through your mind. But you have no other choice than to keep pushing forward.

The most effective way to eliminate this mindset, and start feeling like a busy, successful business owner is to generate more activity. Get yourself in front of more prospects, book more appointments, and grow your client base.

Surely that sounds good to you, right? If not, go ahead and throw away this book right now. There's nothing hear for you. Otherwise, keep reading.

The business world is in some ways the same as it ever was, and in other ways…it's going through massive changes.

What's stayed the same is this: If you want to grow your business, then you need more leads and appointments with qualified prospects. Seems like a no brainer right? Well, it is…except that most small business owners aren't doing anything about it.

For big companies with armies of sales people, this isn't much of a problem. They've got systems in place to generate as many appointments as they can handle.

But the majority of small business owners are con-

stantly on the cash flow roller coaster. One week it feels like you're doing great, and you're busy helping clients...the next you're wondering what happened... and the phone's just not ringing. Where'd all the business go? If you're just getting started, it can feel even worse. Without a track record, it's tough getting people to take you seriously.

Things are changing though, with all of these online tools to attract new leads and book appointments.

This book is the story of how things have changed and what you need to do to take advantage of it, so you can start getting in front of more of your ideal clients.

It's really unfortunate, but the fact is that most people don't know this stuff or are not willing to put in the work. They're either being misled by people with strategies that don't really work for anybody but the person teaching it. Or they're one of the dreamers always looking for a magic bullet, and they're still struggling to grow their own business. The days of the magic bullet are gone, if they ever existed.

To grow your business, it takes work. Period.

You know that already, right? You're willing to do the work. But there is so much confusion out there, that you're not sure where to start. Most small business owners don't have a step-by-step system for generating qualified appointments in place. That's what this book is all about.

And again, this isn't just for big companies. These systems that I'm going to share with you, while they're good for big business too....they were actually designed with the small business in mind. For people just like you and me.

That's what this is really about, bringing the power of big business marketing to OUR kinds of businesses. Putting the power into YOUR hands so you can be the master of your fate. It's in your hands now.

It's about what it really takes to use your computer and an internet connection to generate almost as many leads and appointments as you want, and the incredible opportunity that this represents for the entrepreneur who is ready to seize it. Maybe one just like you.

FOUR

THE BULLSHIT
I WAS FED

We can probably agree on at least one thing:

The internet and the online marketing space is simply way too hypey these days.

If I see another training program that claims to have the key to all of your wildest dreams and riches, the golden ticket to a life of passive income where you sit on the beach and magically make money all day....well, just thinking about it makes me want to throw up in my mouth a little bit. Oh crap, I just did. Hold on, I need to spit this out.

Ok, I'm back.

The serious business owners I work with, they're tired of that crap too. Not only are they tired of it, they've completely tuned it out. They're looking for practical resources to help take what you love to do, to take your business, to the next level. They want, like you, to leverage proven systems for getting in front of more clients, generate more income and revenue, improve your cash flow, and grow your business. And to get a little peace of mind, knowing that you won't have to worry about where your next client will come from.

It's the growth of your business that will allow you to get the lifestyle you want, the ability to make a real difference, and of course...you want to do it without acting like a used car salesman right? You want your business to be something that your friends, family, and you will be proud of. That was huge for me, and still is to this day. I bet it is for you too.

Wait a minute?! Didn't I just tell you that I was sick and tired of hypey pitches that promise you the world and then some? Absolutely. Let's be clear. The system you find in this book is not the answer to all of your wildest dreams. It is a system that will help you generate more leads and appointments. Getting more leads and appointments is ONE critical component of growing your business, and achieving your goals.

Cool? Cool.

So let's talk about the #1 thing that prevents business owners from achieving this. It's what I call, "the cash flow roller coaster," and it's critical to your success that you put the systems in place to get off the roller coaster.

> *The #1 thing that prevents business owners from achieving growth is "the cash flow roller coaster."*

I got my first taste of the cash flow roller coaster back when I was working for my dad. Things were going really well for his business for a long time. Until one day he ran out of work, and was forced to shut his doors. You see, he was on the roller coaster. And maybe you've been there before too.

One month, you feel like you're doing pretty well. So you get busy doing everything except looking for new clients. Then before you know it, the next month comes around, things start slowing down, and because you weren't keeping the pipeline full, now you're almost out of work. Where will your next buck come from?

So how do you prevent this? Well, the answer to that question is also the most proven, time tested strategy for growing any business. And that is… wait for it….

….Getting in front of more prospects!

If you have a system for generating a consistent flow of opportunities and leads, then your business will be very well protected against the roller coaster. You'll be able to grow to the level that you're aiming for.

The key is having a system that attracts your ideal clients, and works them through a process that culminates with them booking a time to speak with you. Whether you call it a consultation, a strategy session, a sales call, or an appointment, we're all talkin' about the same thing.

This is an amazing time to be an entrepreneur because the internet has leveled the playing field for us. With online tools, like email, LinkedIn, and Facebook, you can book appointments with highly targeted prospects. You would never have been able to reach them back in the day, not unless you were a big company that had a massive marketing budget.

Here's the problem. And it's a BIG one. Most of the social media gurus out there, most of their stuff is full of you know what. You probably already know that. Unfortunately, I didn't when I first got started and I had to learn the hard way.

After the failure of the big construction company I worked for, I decided the only option was to work for myself. But I made a promise to myself, that I would never let the same thing happen to my business. That I would always have systems in place to generate as much business as I needed or wanted.

When I first started working for myself, I went out and bought a couple books on using social media to generate business and started following all the big gurus. After all, that's where it's at these days, right? Social media continues to be all the rage, as it was back in 2010.

Using these books, I learned that, supposedly, the best way to get business using social media was to provide value, to be a giver, and above all else…to ENGAGE. Everybody seemed to agree. Engagement was the key. So I tried some of what they recommended. I tried getting involved in conversations, and looking for the right places to strategically add my expertise. Every once in a while, I'd even try to throw in some snarky comments, cause that's what all the cool kids were doing right?

Well, it never seemed to worked for me. In a short amount of time, I realized many of my ideal clients weren't paying attention to these twitter conversations, they weren't following my Facebook business page, and they simply didn't have an interest in my snarky comments. On top of that, I realized that I just wasn't that great at this whole online "engagement" thing. It really seemed like the only people benefiting from all this social media stuff were the people at the top, the people with the big followings.

I continued trying to do what all the gurus said for about 6 months. I got almost nothing out of it, and my new consulting business was sputtering along. In the summer of 2010, I really felt like all of this social media stuff just wasn't for me...and I sure as hell wasn't getting any business from it. So I stopped doing it. Instead, I started using a different approach.

I figured there had to be a SYSTEMATIC approach for generating leads consistently, and without spending any money on advertising. You see, I didn't have a ton of money lying around. I started my business with just a few thousand dollars in the bank. I needed something that would work with just a little elbow grease.

I knew there was a sea of prospects out there, accessible to every one of us. They're just sitting there, waiting for you and for me, but we all know you have to approach them the right way. You have to know the right things to say. Otherwise you won't stand a chance of getting in the door.

I set out to design a system to tap into this sea of prospects. I didn't know it at the time, but that system played on proven psychological triggers, which created the perfect environment for prospects to open up to me. When I combined that with a process for developing targeted contacts into high value prospects, and utilizing a standardized messaging process, things started taking off. I quickly realized that I had a real bonafide system on my hands for generating a predictable number of leads.

Social Media engagement wasn't the answer.

The answer was systematically targeting the right prospects and working them through a process that takes advantage of psychological triggers, to get them to agree to meet with me.

Game on.

FIVE

CAN YOU HELP US WITH THAT?

In a short amount of time, this system was doing more for me than I could have imagined. My client base was growing, and people were considering me one of the top outsourced CFO's in the St. Louis area. They didn't actually know if I was any good or not. They believed I was at the top, simply because I had positioned myself properly.

Call it brand awareness. Call it name recognition. Call it whatever you want. All I know is this. Before this, the leaders in my community hadn't been giving me the time of day. After, I was getting calls and referrals from some of the most respected business people in town. Me, a 29 year old that couldn't even grow a proper moustache, was getting calls from 20 year grizzled business vets, that rarely look outside of the "old boys club."

One story stands out in particular. I had started a LinkedIn group called Small Biz Forum to position my brand and services in front of small business owners. By actively promoting the group in the St. Louis area, I had filled the group with prospective clients. One day, I got a call from a business owner who was a member of the group. He needed help building financial projections for a new venture. I met him at his facility, and his assistant escorted me to his office. He was wrapping up a few things but invited me to have a seat. His computer screen was facing me, and he had Outlook pulled up with his recent emails. I sat patiently, and noticed that the email he currently had selected was the digest of content from my LinkedIn group Small Biz Forum.

Coincidence? Hell no. He had seen my name repeatedly, was receiving the group content, and the day he had a need, I was the one he called. I later found out that I was the only one he called.

This system evolved to include messaging processes, and became so dialed in, I could predict exactly how many appointments I could generate. That's when I knew I had something special.

Having seen the success I was having with this system, I was asked by some of my finance clients if they thought the same marketing and social media processes would work for them.

It was a light bulb moment for me. I realized very few people knew how to do this stuff. They were stuck in the old way of thinking about social media, trying to "engage," and post content hoping somebody would see it. It wasn't working for them either.

I had a hunch that my system could work for almost anybody, so I decided to give it a shot. I brought on my first client in 2011 and attempted to replicate the system for them. We had almost immediate success, and as a direct result of the sales generated through my system, their company has grown significantly in the years since.

I soon realized that helping businesses grow was a real passion of mine, and decided to go full time, leaving the CFO business. Since then, I have been fortunate to serve hundreds of clients around the world in all sorts of industries. From big companies like Microsoft, to small businesses just like mine when I started, and everything in between.

It's proven true. The system works for almost any business.

It can work for you too. If you're ready to put in the work.

Ready?

Let's go!

SIX

THE SYSTEM

In the years since 2011, the system has been tested, refined, and improved upon in many ways. The playbook I'm giving to you, had I known it in its current comprehensive form back when I was starting, would have allowed me to reach even greater heights with my first businesses. I may have found success anyway, but it doesn't always work that way for everybody. I want you to have the greatest chance you possibly can to reach your business goals. The best way to do that is by booking more appointments.

While the system has some moving parts (I'm going to walk you through them), the big picture is this:

Position yourself above the fray, and prospects will be far more approachable than when you're just another me-too competitor in a crowded sea.

When you can position yourself as a leader, as a real expert, your prospects will actually want to talk to you.

Yet using most methods, it can be difficult and very expensive to achieve this kind of "leadership positioning." Even if you have a massive budget, you need leads and clients quickly, right? You don't have the luxury of taking the next couple years to position yourself as a market leader. You need it now. And that is exactly what the Booked system allows you to do.

Booked is a 5-step process that helps you quickly position yourself as an expert in your industry, directly connect you with an unlimited supply of prospects, and work them through processes that will generate a predictable number of leads and appointments. When you have that predictable number of appointments, you'll have a predictable stream of new clients.

Of course, you have to be able to turn an appointment into a client. But even if you only close a small fraction of consultations into clients, the system will work for you. And that's a worst case scenario. For most people I talk to, it's not a matter of being able to close. You've got an amazing service and compelling story, but just aren't getting in front of enough people. Let's change that.

Let me reiterate what this system is one more time:

Booked is a 5-step process that helps you to quickly position yourself as an expert in your industry, directly connect you with an unlimited supply of prospects, and work them through processes that will generate a predictable number of leads and appointments.

That doesn't sound much like the same old social media mumbo jumbo, does it? That's because it's not. While the system does leverage LinkedIn, Facebook, and email, it is not about the platform. It's about the process. No matter where your clients can be found, the process can work for you.

Over the next few chapters I'll walk you through the 5-step process and give you some examples of people who have had amazing success using it.

Step 1

It starts with the foundation. These are the things that you need to put in place FIRST. Without them, the rest of the system will be far less effective.

Step 2

Step two is our proprietary process for quickly establishing your leadership platform. It's this platform that's going to supercharge everything else you do, and it might take you only an hour or two to get up and running.

Step 3

The third step is building your database of prospects. This involves identifying your ideal clients and bringing them into your funnel, in a number of ways, both systematic and free.

Step 4

From there, we'll move to Step 4, your messaging campaign. This is where the results start POURING in. Instead of sitting back and waiting, this proactive approach insures that you'll be generating appointments when you want them.

Step 5

Then in Step 5, learn to combine the systems you've built in Steps 1-4 with email strategies that generate even more appointments. It's funny how so many people get married to one platform. With our system, you'll be leveraging not JUST Facebook. Not JUST LinkedIn. You won't be a one trick pony. You'll be integrating the best of both Facebook and LinkedIn, based on where your target market can best be reached. Then you'll combine them with email to get results that most other people only dream about.

I've said it before and I'll say it again, and again. If you are looking for the easy way out, this is not for you. In my experience, there is no easy way out.

The 'dreamers' are almost never successful. It's the people who are willing to roll up their sleeves, the 'doers', who get real results.

Fortunately, this system doesn't require too much work. It can be managed in under an hour a day.

You can take weekends off too. As long as you are willing to commit to 30-60 minutes a day, 5 days per week, you will get some remarkable results.

SEVEN

THE FOUNDATION

Abraham Lincoln once said, "Give me six hours to chop down a tree, and I will spend the first four sharpening the axe." This system is no different than Abe's tree. If you don't sharpen your axe and put in place the necessary foundational elements first, the rest of it won't be nearly as effective. What we're doing here is building a system that you'll come to rely on for new leads and appointments for years to come. Trying to shortcut the process just isn't worth it.

The first step is clearly identifying who your ideal prospect is. Don't make the mistake of saying "everybody" or "any small business owner."

Trying to be all things to all people leaves your message vanilla, boring, and it won't resonate with anyone.

> *"If you market to everyone as a prospect, you'll get no one as a client." - Virginia Muzquiz*

Your success will improve dramatically when you focus on a specific niche. It might be an industry you've had a lot of success with, or possibly, a specific type of person you like working with. Your niche could be demographic or psychographic. There are entire books on positioning and niche, and we only have a few paragraphs to speak to it here. Regardless, the key at this stage is to get very clear on who your ideal prospect is. Develop a one page cheat sheet including all of the criteria that you will use to find this prospect online.

Prospect Profile Cheat Sheet Basics
Here are some of the common pieces of data that you might include in your prospect profile cheat sheet if you are targeting people in businesses:

- Company Size
- Title
- Geographic Focus

- Seniority
- Male/Female
- Age
- Department or Function

Not going after businesses? Maybe your prospect profile will include information such as:
- Male/Female
- Income Range
- Geographic Focus
- Interests
- Group Associations

These are just samples. Yours may look similar, or quite different. The key is to have a very clear picture of who your ideal client is.

From there, you will be armed with the information you need to create your Prospect Map, which is essentially a roadmap of the places that these prospects hang out in. It could be certain LinkedIn groups, or Facebook groups. Maybe your prospects hang out in niche forums or other communities. Most markets can be found in niche-specific LinkedIn groups, as there are over 1,000,000 of them.

Don't forget to look at Facebook though as certain niches are very well represented on Facebook and are more easily accessed there. Next, start joining these groups.

Once you've identified and begun joining these groups, you need to spend some time understanding what kind of topics interest them and developing your Value Identifiers. These are the things your prospects and clients are interested in, the topics they care about, the stuff they're into, and the things they identify with. A cursory review of the conversations and posts in these groups will give you a good idea of which topics your prospects really care about. What are they asking about? Which discussions seem to have a lot more comments than the others? Create a list of topics that seem to be of interest to your prospects, and set it aside for later. You're going to use this to position yourself as a trusted resource, but let's not get ahead of ourselves. There are still a couple items pieces of our foundation left.

Another awesome approach for getting an understanding of what your prospects care about, is to ask them! Whether through surveys or informal messages, getting direct feedback from your target market is a fantastic way to know exactly what kind of content will attract them. Keep in mind, you won't need to CREATE any of this content.

Optimize Your LinkedIn and/or Facebook Profile(s)

The final component of your foundation is optimizing your LinkedIn and/or Facebook profile(s). Position yourself as a trusted authority in your space, real thought leader. When your prospects check you out, you want them thinking "Oh, this person looks like a peer. A real player in the industry. This is somebody I should connect with." As opposed to "Uh oh, here's somebody that's gonna try to sell me something."

When it comes to LinkedIn profiles, most people talk all about themselves. How great they are, what they do, and so on. Instead, you want to focus on what your prospects care about. More importantly, you want them to feel comfortable connecting with you. Facebook is even easier. You might change your cover photo to include information about your leadership platform (stay tuned for that), or you might leave it just the way it is.

It takes a certain strategic finesse to achieve that this expert effect, but our process systematizes it so that anybody can quickly achieve it. A big key to making it work is the positioning of your leadership platform.

EIGHT

YOUR LEADERSHIP PLATFORM

Your clients are under siege. They're bombarded daily with emails, ads, and messages from businesses trying to sell them something. Like a pesky mosquito buzzing around their face, these advertising messages leave them wanting to do nothing less than SMACK! If you think all it takes to book some appointments is to pile on with everybody else, think again. You'll be just the next in line to get smashed and left for dead.

The key to getting a foot in the door, is to position yourself as somebody they know, like, and trust. People do business with people they have relationships with. If you want to generate more appointments, you need to develop more relationships.

The Booked system is a step-by-step process for achieving that. It starts with building a leadership platform.

Developing Your Leadership Platform

At a high level, the plan is to set yourself apart from your competitors. Without this, the other strategies in this system won't be as effective. You begin developing this platform by owning a targeted group full of your ideal prospects. You can't just be another Joe Schmoe.

Consider a financial advisor who reaches out to a prospect to line up a phone call or coffee. The prospect is thinking "I've seen a million of you guys, I don't need to talk to another one." When you are the founder of a community targeted to those prospects, people are much more open to your advances. And you'll get better results.

Let's say you're in the business of selling software or services to construction companies, specifically commercial construction firms. Imagine now that you're the founder of "The Commercial Construction Leadership Network" on LinkedIn. With that intro, prospects will recognize you as a leader in the industry. It might seem simple, but the impact it has on your ability to get people to open up to you, is profound.

To achieve this effect, you'll need to create your group on either Facebook or LinkedIn. They're the most popular online networks, and we'll talk in a moment about which might be best for you.

Our primary focus for this leadership platform is to generate appointments. It's also great for the secondary purposes of general marketing, brand awareness, content distribution, driving traffic, and more.

It takes a bit of time to set up, but once it's up and running, it will take very little of your time. Now, you might decide you want to spend more time managing your group, but it's not necessary. The main consideration is simply that you are running the group, and the positioning that goes with it. Make sure to adjust your profile slightly on both Facebook and LinkedIn, to make it clear that you are the founder of your group.

LinkedIn or Facebook?

Some markets are better for Facebook, some for LinkedIn. Referring back to your ideal prospect profile, you need to be clear about whether your prospects are more likely to engage on Facebook or LinkedIn. Let's say you're targeting CEO's of manufacturing companies. They're not likely to engage in a business conversation on Facebook. You'll want to focus more on LinkedIn.

But let's say you're going after people in marketing, business coaches, or b2c (business to consumer). Then Facebook could be the right play for you. It just depends on your target market. Your initial research in phase 1 ("The Foundation") should have made this pretty clear, as you already identified the places your prospects are hanging out.

In some cases, it's easier to grow your LinkedIn group initially, if you don't already have an audience. That's because you can perform the database build, create your database in LinkedIn, and then invite all of those new connections to join your group. You're virtually guaranteed to succeed quickly.

Facebook can take a bit more time, if you don't currently have an audience. However, you can use that same LinkedIn database and invite these LinkedIn connections to your Facebook group. This can be beneficial because prospects are a bit easier to identify on LinkedIn. You can do prospecting on Facebook, but it's much more limited, and building a large database on Facebook takes more time. Thus, we often recommend that you start with LinkedIn, even if your group is going to be on Facebook.

Personal chefs are a great example. You can find 12,000+ personal chefs on LinkedIn. Even though they may not spend much time on LinkedIn, you'll connect with them on LinkedIn as the first step. Then once you're connected on LinkedIn, you'll invite them back to the Facebook group.

We'll be talking more about the database build process in the next chapter. It boils down to this: You want your group to be in place before you perform your database build, so you can leverage the positioning to increase the response rate. When you're reaching out to prospects, they'll see that you are the founder of your group, giving you instant positioning and credibility. Doing this, you'll quickly have hundreds of new prospects in your database who view you as a leader. And a marketing asset that will churn out leads for years.

NINE

BUILDING YOUR DATABASE

Now that you've got your foundation in place and your leadership platform is set up, you're probably wondering, "Where are all the prospects?" Knowing how to find your best prospects and ideal clients, and how to connect with them, is the next step.

We call it "Building Your Database" because that's what it is. It's a real database of prospects that you'll be able to nurture and turn into qualified leads for years to come. There are really two phases to the process for building your database. The first is an initial blitz where you'll reach out to hundreds of prospects. The second phase is where you'll continue growing the database by regularly reaching out to new prospects on an ongoing basis. This second phase essentially never ends, as we recommend reaching out to at least a few new prospects every day. Well, not every day. You can take the weekend off if you'd like.

There is a very systematic way to do this. When done correctly, you'll attract hundreds of targeted prospects into your network overnight. Like I said in the last chapter, the database build comes after your leadership platform, in the form of a LinkedIn or Facebook group, is in place.

Let's look at an example. Bob Cherry is the owner of Cherry Consulting Group, LLC. He's a management consultant specializing in the oil & gas industry. Currently, Bob's LinkedIn headline reads "President, Cherry Consulting Group, LLC." When Bob reaches out to a prospect, they're going to check out his profile. When they see this, they'll be immediately thinking "Uh oh, Bob's gonna try and sell me something." Naturally, the response rate will be very low.

Luckily for Bob, he found this book and, after using the Booked system, he recently launched a LinkedIn group called "Oil & Gas Executive Network." At the same time, he changed his headline to read "Founder, Oil & Gas Executive Network." Now when a prospect views Bob's profile, they view him as a peer and a leader in the industry. They're much more open to connecting. That one little change opens the doors to some of the most senior decision makers that Bob has never before been able to get through to.

That's the power of this strategy, and it works regardless of your market or niche. Whether you're targeting c-level hot shots at big companies, small business owners, marketers, retirees, holistic healers, you name it. The power is in creating a community that's all about your prospects.

Once your LinkedIn and/or Facebook profiles are positioned properly, now it's time to begin the Database Build. Again, whether you will be reaching out to prospects on LinkedIn or Facebook (or both) depends on your business, your target market, and where your prospects can best be reached. Let's look at LinkedIn first.

Building a Database on LinkedIn

Performing an initial database build on LinkedIn requires simply sending connection requests to a large number of targeted prospects. You'll use the advanced people search (LinkedIn's search tool) to find qualified prospects and send them a connection request. You'll want to send at least 300 connection requests in the initial database build. If you really want to go all out, you can send up to 1,500.

You might be thinking at this point, "Yeah, but Josh, am I allowed to connect with all of these people if I don't really know them?" Yes. The key is including a personalized script in the connection request. Sticking with the stock script from LinkedIn is a mistake, and your response rate will go way down. Using a personalized script will typically get 50-70% of prospects to connect with you.

Here's a simple example of what this script might look like:

Hey First Name,

I came across your profile here on LinkedIn and thought we could benefit from being connected.

Thanks!

Your Name
Founder, Your Group Name

It will take you a few hours to complete this phase of the system, but you'll pick up a large number of new connections very quickly. This will give you a tremendous database to launch your ongoing appointment generating campaign. And this is just the initial database build!

Building a Database on Facebook

Let's talk about Facebook now. Connecting with prospects on Facebook is a bit different. For one, it is not as easy to search for prospects, and therefor is more difficult to find them. One way around this is to join the groups they hang out in. If you're looking to reach business coaches, find marketing or coaching groups. By joining these groups, you'll have access to hundreds or thousands of prospects. The alternative is to identify them in other places (like LinkedIn) and then search for them by name on Facebook.

Let's say you're looking to get in front of Dentists in the Chicago area. You know they are on Facebook. (If you're doubting that fact, all I can say is that you just need to trust me. Everybody is on Facebook. Everybody.) It's just a matter of finding them. You first need to know their name in order to look them up on Facebook. So how do we do that? Search for Dentists in Chicago on LinkedIn! Then, take the prospect list from LinkedIn, and search for them individually on Facebook.

From there, you'll want to take a two step process to becoming Facebook friends.

Step 1 is to send them a message. The message could be something such as

Hi First Name,

I came across your info here and thought it wouldn't hurt to reach out! I'm the founder of the Dentistry Leadership Forum. Maybe we can benefit from being connected here.

Thanks!

Or, if you found them in a group, the message might say

Hey First Name,

we're both in the National Association of Dentists Group and I thought it wouldn't hurt to reach out. I'm the founder of the Dentistry Leadership Forum. Maybe we can benefit from being connected here.

Thanks!

Step 2 is to follow up with a friend request. You might be thinking, "Josh, come on buddy. COME ON BUDDY! People don't like talkin' business on Facebook. This is about as silly as a red-headed pecker willow on a Tuesday morning." You'd be wrong. It's a numbers game. A large percentage of these people will agree to be friends with you because of the way you framed the introduction. Some people just like having more friends, and others will want to connect with you because they perceive you to be a leader in the market, from your well positioned leadership platform.

With Facebook, we recommend proceeding with a bit more caution in terms of the number of friend requests you send at once. You probably don't want to send more than 100 per day, in the beginning. It's also important that each message not be a carbon copy of the next. If Facebook thinks you're spamming people, they could restrict your account. You can avoid that by making sure each message is a little bit different than the next. A couple tweaks to the wording will do the trick. Better safe than sorry with these things.

Just like the LinkedIn process, doing an initial database build on Facebook can give you a solid foundation of hundreds of new prospects to begin working through the system. And this is just the beginning! Are you ready for hundreds of new prospects to line up phone calls and meetings with? It's only days away!

As I mentioned, the second phase includes ongoing prospecting and outreach. We recommend reaching out to 5 new prospects every single day as part of your ongoing marketing plan. This will provide you with a steady stream of new prospects being added into your leadership platform, as well as directly connecting with you. Using our proprietary messaging processes, you'll be armed with a weapon that will convert a predictable number of these prospects into live appointments, consultations, and strategy sessions.

Real World Examples

Looking for examples of real world businesses like yours that have implemented these strategies? Sign up for your free video training at:

TheBookedBook.com/Videos

In addition to more in-depth training on the topics covered in this book, you'll also find case studies for businesses in a wide range of industries.

TEN

YOUR MESSAGING MACHINE

If all you implemented were the first 3 phases of the system that we covered so far, you'd be ahead of 90% of your competitors. Stopping there would be doing yourself a disservice, because there is a way to take it to the next level and to generate a consistent stream of new appointments.

How many new appointments do you need to reach your goals? Some people might need only a few more each month. Others might be looking for 20 each week.

Don't worry about what you think other people are doing. Figure out how many prospects YOU need to reach YOUR goals.

The best way to determine that is to do a quick ROI calculation. How much additional income do you need to bring in? How many new clients will it take to achieve that? Let's assume it's 5 new clients per month. Now, consider how many prospects you need to meet with in order to sign 5 new clients. If you REALLY know your numbers, it's easy to answer that question.

If you're not sure, come up with a good ballpark. Make it conservative though. Too many people overestimate their sales effectiveness. Think you can close 50%? Let's get conservative and make that number 20%. Sound way too low? Great! It's an awesome feeling to exceed your goals.

Assuming you need 5 new clients a month, at 20% close rate, you'll need to generate 25 appointments per month. That's roughly 6 appointments per week. Now you have a metric that you can track. A popular saying in business is "you manage what you measure." It's true. If you're just shootin' in the dark, your results will be all over the place. When you have clear goals to track against, you can hold yourself accountable and increase the chances that you'll hit your income goals.

Now that you're clear on your goals, let's get down to the nitty gritty. How are we actually going to generate these appointments?

By simply launching and managing your Facebook or LinkedIn group, you will generate leads and appointments passively. In other words, your new friends, connections, and group members will sometimes reach out to you to talk business without you having to do anything. Why? Because you're the leader now, and they have a need.

Yet, these passive "inbound" leads typically won't add up to enough to meet your weekly goal for new appointments. To bridge the gap, you need a proactive approach for funneling these prospects into appointments. We facilitate this steady flow of new appointments with messaging campaigns.

Since 2008, my team and I have been testing and refining different processes and scripts. These processes require being proactive and regularly reaching out to your best prospects to invite them to a phone call or meeting. If you want to just sit back and see what comes your way, that's fine. But keep in mind, that's what most people do. Most people are not generating the kinds of results you're looking for. Why do you think companies like Microsoft have hired us to install this system for their teams? They know the most time-tested, proven way to grow is to go out, position yourself in front of your prospects, and ask for the meeting.

Sitting back and hoping is NOT a plan.

I want you to draw a line in the sand and commit to doing the work it's going to take to get you the kind of results you want. The best way to do that is through proactive outreach, not through soft and fluffy social media stuff. What we're talking about is a systematic process for working prospects through direct outreach and messaging campaigns that are going to get you lots of appointments.

There are a number of different types of campaigns we teach. Each of them gets a different response rate on average, and each has a different purpose and time when you might want to use it.

A few of the messaging campaign processes we teach our students include:

- Multi-Touch Point Nurture Campaign
- Referencing a Shared Connection
- Request for Call Right After Connecting
- Re-engaging Existing Connections
- Asking Permission to Send Your Lead Magnet

These are five of our most effective approaches, but there are many more we have implemented for our clients and recommend to our students. These five are a great start. Additionally, each of these approaches does not live on an island. They can be combined to achieve even greater effectiveness. The key is in the strategic design of a messaging system that will work well for you and be effective for your target market. This "strategic design" is a bit of a nuanced skill, but with practice and testing you can find a mix that will generate amazing results and tons of appointments. Or, you can shortcut the process and work with my team to coach you through the process.

Let's discuss each messaging process in a bit more detail.

Multi-Touch Point Nurture Campaign
The multi-touch point nurture campaign has historically been the most effective messaging process in our arsenal. On average, 29% of prospects worked

through the process will agree to a phone call with you, on average. In some markets it has been lower, and in others higher. Regardless, the bottom line is that it works.

This process involves sending a minimum of 4-5 messages over the course of 2-3 months. Each message is sent 2-3 weeks apart. The first 2-3 messages are simply meant to develop the relationship and position you as somebody your prospects can trust. The last two messages are where you go for the phone call or meeting.

You're already seen as a leader in your prospect's eyes, as a result of your leadership platform. Because of the quality content that you'll drip out from this platform, these prospects will be seeing your name on a regular basis and in a very positive way. Now you're going to supercharge it by working them through a 1-on-1 messaging process.

The first message is typically just to thank them for connecting and to let them know you look forward to keeping in touch. You may also mention something to the effect of "If there's anything I can help you with, don't hesitate to ask!" The second message should include a piece of awesome content you think they'd be interested in. This should be something you DID NOT create. Instead, you want this to be an article or resource written by a third party. There's nothing in it for you. You're just sharing it with your new friend, because you think they'll get value out of it. It can be as simple as saying,

Hey Bobby,

I came across this case study and thought of you. Really smart how they are using X to get new X. Thought you'd be interested in it too. Hope you're doing well!

Your Name

Then, the third message might be calling their attention to a discussion happening in your group.

Hey Bobby,

There's a discussion happening in the [group name] group that I thought you'd want to check out. Would love your thoughts on this: [link to discussion]

Thanks!

These first three messages simply serve to nurture the relationship and share valuable resources with your prospects. This gets them engaged with you and if done strategically, gets them thinking about your solutions in a way that doesn't feel pushy.

Now it's time to ask for the phone call. The fourth message might look like this:

Bobby

We've been keeping in touch here for the last few weeks, and as much as I love all this social media stuff...I still like to get to know my connections in the real world. Would you be open to a no-agenda call to see how we might be able to help each other? How does next Tuesday afternoon look?

Your Name

You'll get a lot of bites. But don't stop there!

Too many people throw in the towel after one message, but you know better than that. You know that follow up and persistence is the key to maximizing your results. And you've probably heard that it takes at least 7 touches before getting through to a prospect. Some people say 12 touches, and honestly, I've heard all sorts of numbers. No matter what it is, we can all agree that the more touches you make, the greater your chances of success.

The next message is a simple follow-up. Nothing more than:

Hey Bobby,

Just following up on the last message I sent you.
Would love to get a call set up if you're open to it.
Let me know!

Your Name

Between the final 2 messages requesting a phone call, we've seen (on average) 29% of prospects agree to the phone call. Using that average, you'd need to add about 86 prospects through the process each month to arrive at 25 appointments per month.

Are you starting to see how systematic this is? This is the kind of system I envisioned when I first started my business, and realized that most of the other stuff out there just wasn't working for me. One of the most important things to keep in mind is that each of these communications is sent one-on-one. Each message is personalized with the prospect's first name. Yet, you're sending the same copy to each prospect as you work batches of prospects through your ongoing messaging campaigns. This is the kind of "engagement" that worked for me, and we've found that it works for almost any type of business.

But like I said, the "Multi-Touch Point Messaging

Campaign" is just one approach. Let's spend a bit of time talking about the rest.

Referencing a Shared Connection

When I ask most business owners, "Where are you currently getting most of your business?" I hear time and time again: Referrals. There is no doubt that referrals produce some of the best leads money can buy. Yet for most, relying solely on referrals is a recipe for lackluster performance. You're simply not getting enough of them to reach your goals.

But what if you could leverage the power of referrals and shared relationships to generate more leads… without actually having somebody else make the referral? That's what this process does. I'm not claiming that this approach is equal to a legitimate referral. It's not. That said, we're leveraging the same psychological triggers to get you in the door with more prospects.

This process involves identifying prospects you have a second degree LinkedIn connection or mutual Facebook friend with. Both groups of people are one degree removed from you, meaning that you share at least one common connection. There are a couple ways to leverage these points of commonalty.

For one, you can leverage the relationship in your initial outreach. When sending a friend or connection request, personalize the message you send to reference the shared connection.

Hey Bobby,

I saw that we're both connected to Ben Gahlken and thought it wouldn't hurt to reach out. Would love to connect here if you're open to it!

Your Name

You'll get an extremely high acceptance rate using this approach.

Another way to leverage these common connections is to go straight for the appointment. The approach might look something like this:

Hey Bobby,

I saw that we're both connected to Ben Gahklen and thought it wouldn't hurt to reach out. Ben and I have done a lot of networking over the years and I've really valued the connections he's made. Would love to jump on a call and learn more about what you're doing, and how we might be able to help each other. How does Tuesday at 3:00 Eastern work for you?

Thanks!

You might be reading this and thinking to yourself, "Why wouldn't I just do this? Why go through the effort of the Multi-Touch Point campaign when I can just ask for the appointment right away?" Because the response rate will be lower.

In almost every campaign we've tested, asking for an appointment before you get to know somebody results in a lower acceptance rate.

Sometimes significantly lower. So why am I recommending this approach to you? Because rules are meant to be broken. What doesn't work for others may work well for you. Most importantly, you may need to generate appointments more quickly than the Multi-Touch Point campaign allows. If you need to get some appointments on the calendar, while the long term nurture strategy builds up, the process we just discussed can be a nice thing to do in the meantime. Just keep in mind that you will burn through more prospects, so be sure to track your results.

Request for Call Right After Connecting

Another approach for generating calls more quickly is to connect, and then ask for the phone call. This approach is pretty simple. First, send a connection or friend request. Once they accept, send a message asking them if they'd be open to jumping on a call to learn more about each other.

The script might look like this:

Hey Bobby,

Thanks for connecting! As much as I love all this social media stuff, I still like to get to know my connections in the real world. Let me know if you'd be open to jumping on a call to learn more about what you're up to. I've got some ideas on how we might be able to do some things together. How does next Tuesday look?

Your Name

Be prepared to send a follow up message or two in case they don't respond right away. Give them a few days before following up again, you don't want to seem too eager. As with the "shared connection" approach, this process will usually generate a lower response rate than the Multi-Touch Point campaign. That said, in certain cases we've actually seen it perform better. It all depends on your target market, and to some extent your business and how unique it is. If you have something really special, prospects will agree to speak with you at a higher rate. This "request a call immediately after connecting" approach is another good way to generate appointments in the short term while you wait for the nurture campaign to reach its peak.

Re-engaging Existing Connections

Many of our clients and students start with an existing base of prospects to market to. Maybe you've built up a few hundred connections on LinkedIn that look like good prospects, but it's been a long time since you engaged with them in any way. Is there a way to re-engage these old connections? Absolutely!

For starters, you'll want to invite them to join your new leadership platform (your Facebook or LinkedIn group). This is a great first step to getting them back in the loop. From there, you can work them through the rest of the system just as you will with new prospects. That said, there's another approach you can take to move these prospects toward an appointment, sooner rather than later.

Typically you want to acknowledge that it's been a while since you last connected or spoke, and thought it might be a good time to catch up. The message might look something like this:

> *Hey Bobby,*
>
> *I was going through some of my contacts and your name popped up. Can't believe it's been so long since we connected {or met, or spoke}! I'd love to jump on a call and catch up and hear what you've been up to, if you're open to it? How does next Tuesday afternoon look?*
>
> *Looking forward to it!*
>
> *Your Name*

Even if the prospect doesn't respond to this message, don't give up. Of course you should send a follow up message. If they don't respond to the follow up either, then you might decide to move them into a more long term monthly drip campaign, or transition them into a Multi-Touch Point campaign. As always, keep in mind that it's a numbers game. The more touch points you make with every prospect, the more appointments and sales you're going to make.

Asking Permission to Send Your Lead Magnet

I love this approach. Here we're going to utilize a special piece of content, a lead magnet, or possibly a case study. But instead of sending them to an opt-in page where the prospect has to enter their email, we're just going to send it to them.

> *These days, landing pages and funnels and conversion tracking are all the rage. We sometimes forget that keeping it simple is also a very viable option.*

With this approach, simplicity can significantly improve your results. The first message looks something like this:

Hey Bobby,

We've been connected here for a while and I thought you might be interested in a new report I'm putting together. It's all about how {avatar, type of company, etc} can {benefit} by {thing you do}. I'd love to send you a copy. Would you prefer I send it here on LinkedIn, or would email be better?

Notice how you're not sending them a link to a landing page. You're asking permission to send them the report. When they say yes, send them a link straight to the download for the report. Boom!

But what about those who don't respond? Send a follow up! In this case, I like to assume the sale and just send them the report.

Hey Bobby,

Just following up on my message from last week. Didn't hear back from you but I assume you're super busy, so I'll just link up the report here. You can download it here: <link> There's no opt in required and nothing to buy. Just thought you could get some good value out of it. Let me know what you think!

Thanks,

Your Name

Now it's sitting right there in their inbox, and a very high percentage of people will click through and check it out. If the content in the report is decent, it will serve to increase their interest in your services.

From there, send them a third message a week later.

Hi Bobby,

Just wanted to follow up on the report I sent you last week. Hopefully you've had a chance to check it out. In any event, I'd love to jump on a call some time and learn more about the work you're doing. Happy to answer any questions you have about the ideas in the report. How does next Tuesday afternoon look?

Thanks!

If they don't respond to this message, send another follow up.

There are many different ways to utilize a lead magnet or case study inside of messaging campaigns. This is just one approach. You might also consider adding a message into the Multi-Touch Point campaign, and you can also periodically promote your lead magnet inside of your group.

Which Approach Is Best For You?

I've given you five different approaches to consider. Any one of them can create great results, but obviously you can't use them all at the same time for the same batch of prospects. So which should you start with?

The first step is creating a messaging campaign playbook. This is the calendar of activity, and a summary of what's going to happen. These campaigns can include a number of details that have to be tracked, and it's important that you have it planned out and well organized. You'll want to include information regarding the message timing/date and the message script that was used.

The messaging scripts you use will vary. As I mentioned, we have a number of processes we teach our students. The key is to find a process that will warm up your prospects, build some trust, and then once that trust is established, go for the appointment. You'll probably want to start by adding a batch of prospects into the Multi-Touch Point campaign. Concurrently you can work a different batch of prospects through one of the other approaches. This way you'll have different prospects being worked through different campaigns, which will result in a steady flow of leads.

It's critical that you also have a system for tracking the prospects through your campaign. When following our system, you'll have hundreds of prospects in your funnel. If you're not well organized, things will inevitably slip through the cracks and you'll miss out on opportunities. Some of the basic information you'll want to track includes name, email, phone number (if you have it), company name, other notes, and details about which messages and campaigns have been sent.

At this point you might be thinking, "wait a minute

Josh, did you just say HUNDREDS of prospects? Won't messaging that many people individually take a ton of time?" Great question! Fortunately there are easy ways to make the process very efficient. Sure, you will definitely spend a few minutes each day sending out messages. There's no way around that, unless your comfortable with mediocre results. Sending personalized 1-on-1 messages dramatically improves the response rate and effectiveness of the system. One of the reasons it works so well is that a lot of people simply aren't willing to put it in the time to do it! When you start seeing the leads pour in, you'll be glad you took the time to do it the right way.

But there's one more thing that you can do to improve your results even further, and book even more appointments. Email.

ELEVEN

EMAIL BLUEPRINT

Adding good ol' fashioned email into the mix is a surefire way to improve your results. Some of the prospects you connect with on LinkedIn and Facebook may not be paying constant attention to their inboxes on these social networks. But you better believe they're looking at their email! In fact, a recent study out of the University of British Columbia revealed that the average person checks their email 15 times a day. There's just no other way around it. Email is one of the best places to reach your prospects.

You can get excellent results with the system, even if you do not integrate email into your approaches. Yet with email, your results will increase. It's like anything in marketing. The more places you can reach your prospects where they're hanging out, the better your odds of booking an appointment with them. We know they're probably on LinkedIn, and we know they're probably on Facebook. But we know without a doubt that they are spending lots of time in their email inbox. So why not show up there too?

Before I share a couple strategies with you, I want to clarify what we're NOT talking about here. When you think about email in the context of marketing to your prospects, it's natural to immediately consider email marketing software such as MailChimp, Aweber, Infusionsoft, etc. These tools are fantastic for permission-based marketing where prospects opt-in to your list, and you send them periodic marketing emails. They're sent in bulk. You set up the email, and with a few clicks, it sends an automated email to every one of your prospects. If they no longer receive value from your emails, they can click the unsubscribe button and never hear from you again. This is not the kind of email we're talking about.

I am not recommending that you add people to your mailchimp (or whatever software you use for email marketing) and start sending broadcasts to them without permission. Nobody likes that.

Instead, what we've seen work tremendously is to layer individual email outreach on top of the messaging campaigns you run within LinkedIn and Facebook.

For our purposes here, we're not importing prospects into email marketing software. The messages we send will be 1-to-1, personalized messages. There is no unsubscribe button. These emails look like something you'd send to a friend, and because of that, they get a great response rate. There are two approaches to consider, as it relates to converting prospects you've identified into appointments on your calendar.

Think about it this way. If you send a prospect a couple messages on LinkedIn, and they don't respond, should you give up? Take your ball and go home? No! Maybe they didn't receive your message, or maybe it got overlooked. Or, maybe they just don't check LinkedIn that often! By simply sending them an email saying "Hey, just want to make sure you saw my message on LinkedIn..." you'll get a ton of responses from prospects.

Knowing that, why not systematize it? That's what the email blueprint is all about.

And, it's 100% CAN-SPAM compliant. Meaning

that this kind of email is most certainly not SPAM. Think of it as following up with a friend. It's essentially the same thing.

Certainly you can use email to send cold messages. In fact, we've had tremendous success using cold email to generate leads and appointments. Sometimes we teach some of these methods to our students. But what we're really focused on here is using email in conjunction with a social messaging campaign.

It works like this. After you send the scripted messages in your Facebook or LinkedIn messaging campaign, then filter your tracking list and make sure to remove those who responded. Move those who didn't respond over to the email campaign, and send a couple new messages there. It's this persistent follow up that generates the greatest results. Not everybody will respond right away. Sometimes it takes a few tries. And remember, we're not humping legs here. These messages are designed to add value to your prospect's world. Not to harass them about taking an appointment with you.

A well designed email campaign can add 10-20% response rate to the overall system. Over time, that's a tremendous amount of additional appointments that you don't want to miss out on!

Want a Free Blueprint of the Booked Appointment Generation System?

To support you in implementing these ideas, I've created a supplementary one-page infographic that maps out the various steps involved in building your appointment generating system.

Having this visual aid will greatly help your understanding and implementation of the system. And I want you to have it for free, so I've included it with the complimentary video training series.

To claim your copy, visit:

TheBookedBook.com/Videos

TWELVE

ONWARD!

I've given you a lot to process so far in this book. Your head is probably swimming with possibilities at this point, and I bet you're wondering what the best process is for moving forward. Let's do a quick recap, and then discuss the keys to actually getting it done and generating more appointments and new business.

We've covered the foundation, the things you need to put in place first to insure that you get the very best results and put your best foot forward. I showed you the secrets to developing an Authority Leadership Platform that will position you as true leader in your market, creating authority that will open prospects up to you like never before. From there, I showed you the best practices for prospecting and building a database of targeted potential clients. Then we gave you an overview of five of our most effective messaging processes that you'll use to convert a percentage of the prospects in your database into appointments on your calendar. And finally, the email blueprint to improve your results even more.

It's a lot to take in all at once. Fortunately, there's a step-by-step process for building out your entire appointment generating system in just a few weeks. I've eluded to the students and clients my company serves a few times, so you probably assumed that my company offers training to help business owners implement these strategies. You assumed correct.

We've helped over 6,000 businesses implement these systems, and along the way have been perfecting every step of the process. Our flagship training program, The Appointment Generator, provides step-by-step instruction on the entire system as well as 1-on-1 support to insure that our students succeed. You can find more information and join the program at TheAppointmentGenerator.com

After helping so many businesses implement this system, we've found that there are a few keys to successfully implementing and managing the process, so that you get the results you're after…lots of appointments with qualified prospects!

One key is building a calendar of activity. There are a number of moving parts in the system. If I told you it was so simple a monkey could do it; that would be an insult to your intelligence. There is some complexity here. One way to bring some clarity to the process is to organize your action items into a calendar. We find that it is very helpful to plan 2 months ahead at a time.

By planning in advance, you realize a couple of key benefits. For one, you'll have every day planned out. You'll know exactly which tasks to complete, each and every day. Have you ever sat in front of your computer and wondered, "What am I supposed to be doing?!" We've all been there. That's why we help our students put a complete task list together for every step of the process and then schedule every day in advance.

The second benefit of planning your tasks in advance is that you can estimate exactly when your appointments will start being booked, and how many. You'll be able to see the dates that certain messages will be sent. Based on historical percentages, you can predict approximately how many appointments the different messages will generate. That way, you can easily throttle your activity up or down, to arrive at the precise number of appointments that you're aiming to generate. Compare that with what you're currently doing. I bet it's night and day.

Another key to successfully implementing the Booked system is to put in the time. It should go without saying, but again, there is no easy button. I don't know of any systems for generating new clients and sales in your business that don't require putting in some work. That said, the beauty of this system is that you can reach a large number of highly targeted prospects, and you can do it efficiently. I won't even ask you to work on the weekend!

How much time should you expect to devote to this? At least 20 minutes per day, 5 days per week. It will take more time to get things set up over the first few weeks. Once you're foundation is in place, your leadership platform is up and running, and you've got your initial database build completed, you can achieve great results on just 30 minutes per day, 5 days per week. If you want to implement every step of the process and generate the best results possible, you'll want to devote an hour per day. For most people, that's the maximum amount of time you could spend. So, somewhere between 30-60 minutes is the sweet spot.

Many of our students tell me that this is some of the most fun 30-60 minutes of their day. The main reason for that is that they have a daily action plan. This time isn't spent wandering aimlessly around the web. It's laser focused. You'll pull up your action plan for the day, work through the short list of activities that need to be completed that day. Then you're done for the day. You can rest assured that you're finally spending time using social media in an effective manner, generating new appointments and sales.

THIRTEEN

GETTING OFF THE CASH FLOW ROLLERCOASTER

The cash flow rollercoaster is the leading cause of death for businesses. Without consistent cash flow, you're only one downturn away from being out of business. The way to get off the rollercoaster is to have a steady stream of new opportunities and clients. The way to insure that happens, is to have a system for generating a consistent flow of new leads and appointments.

If you want to maximize the impact you are making in the world, and you want the freedom that's supposed to come with running your own business, you need to start getting in front of more prospects. You need a system for positioning yourself as a leader in your market, so you're not just another "me too" competitor. And you must be willing to put in the time to work the processes that I've laid out for you in this book.

Only a small percentage of people who read this book will actually take action on these ideas and this systems.

I want you to be one of the few that decides that NOW is the time to make a change.

Are you with me? It's right there in front of you. Maybe you're looking to add just a few more clients to your business, or maybe you're looking to pick up a few new clients each week. Whatever your goals, it's simply a matter of resolving to do it, putting one foot in front of the other, and starting.

You're about to change your business forever. Your journey is just beginning.

RESOURCES TO HELP YOU BOOK MORE APPOINTMENTS

My company offers a number of resources to help you implement the Booked system:

Booked Companion Video Series

We've develop a complimentary series of videos to guide you through the system outlined in this book. It's free, and also includes complimentary resources to help you even further.

Get yours now at:
TheBookedBook.com/Videos

The Booked Appointment Generation Blueprint

To help support you in implementing the Booked system, we've put together a blueprint outlining the different steps in the process. This visual guide maps out the steps necessary to get your appointment generating system up and running.

It's part of the video training series that you can get free at:
TheBookedBook.com/Videos

Booked in Action - Real World Examples

Looking for examples of real world businesses like yours that have implemented these strategies? In addition to more in-depth training on the topics covered in this book, you'll find case studies for businesses in a wide range of industries at:
TheBookedBook.com/Videos

The Appointment Generator Advanced Training Program

Our critically acclaimed training program, The Appointment Generator, provides you with everything you need to implement the ideas and systems presented in this book. When you join, you'll learn:

- How to setup your foundation, including

 **92**

development of your prospect profile, market research, and all necessary setup items.

- How to build, launch, and manage your Leadership Authority Platform.
- Use the step-by-step process for quickly building a massive database.
- How to design and execute messaging campaigns that generate a consistent flow of new leads and appointments.
- The proven scripts (over 20 pages) you'll use to attract qualified prospects into your network, and then working them all the way to the appointment.
- How to integrate your LinkedIn and Facebook efforts with email, to increase your appointments by 10-20%.
- The daily step-by-step action plan, so you'll know exactly what to do, every single day.

When you join The Appointment Generator, you'll be assigned a dedicated coach to help you work through the program. And we guarantee results.

For more details and to join, visit:
TheAppointmentGenerator.com

Additional Resources

You can find more marketing and entrepreneurship articles and resources by visiting my company blog at LinkedSelling.com, as well as my personal blog at JoshTurner.me. Both sites have a wealth of information, and even more free bonuses for you.

ABOUT
JOSH TURNER

Josh Turner is the Wall Street Journal bestselling author of Connect, and the Founder & CEO of Linked
Selling, a B2B marketing firm specializing in fully
outsourced LinkedIn lead generation campaigns.
They represent clients (like Neil Patel and Microsoft,
to name a couple) in the US, Canada, UK, Asia, and
Australia, in a wide variety of industries. Josh is also
the creator of Linked University and The Appointment Generator training programs, which have
together served over 6,000 entrepreneurs. He lives
in St. Louis with his long-time girlfriend, Jess, and
their dog, Oscar (aka Buddy).

You can send Josh an email and say hi at
Josh@LinkedSelling.com

Made in the USA
Middletown, DE
04 May 2016

JUL — - 2016'